**FRIENDS
OF ACPL**

P9-DYP-174

Sea Queens
Women Pirates
Around the World

JANE YOLEN

Illustrated by Christine Joy Pratt

Charlesbridge

This book is for the pirate princesses I love:
Glendon Callan-Piatt, Maddison Stemple-Piatt,
Alison Stemple, the twins Caroline and Amelia Stemple—
and their moms, Heidi, Betsy, and Joanne Stemple—J. Y.

For Roxy Lee Lawena Burke,
Hawai'i, 21st century—C. J. P.

Published by Charlesbridge
85 Main Street
Watertown, MA 02472
(617) 926-0329
www.charlesbridge.com

Library of Congress Cataloging-in-Publication Data
Yolen, Jane.
    Sea queens : women pirates around the world / Jane Yolen ; illustrated by
Christine Joy Pratt.
        p. cm.
Includes bibliographical references and index.
    ISBN 978-1-58089-131-8 (reinforced for library use)
1. Women pirates—History. 2. Women pirates—Biography. I. Pratt,
Christine Joy. II. Title.
G535.Y65 2008
910.4'5—dc22   2007026983

Printed in China
(hc) 10 9 8 7 6 5 4 3 2 1

Illustrations done in pen and ink on scratchboard
Display type set in P22 Mayflower and text type set in Goudy
Color separations by Chroma Graphics, Singapore
Printed and bound by Jade Productions
Production supervision by Brian G. Walker
Designed by Susan Mallory Sherman and Martha MacLeod Sikkema

Contents

Sea Queens
Women Pirates
Around the World

The Sea Queens

A pirate is a robber who roams the oceans of the world. He thieves and pillages and murders. Above his ship flies the skull-and-crossbones flag.

The pirate is a low-class dog, a dirty down-and-outer with few teeth and a black patch on his eye. He is as often dead drunk as sober.

But wait—not all of that is true.

Some pirates did their thieving on rivers.

Some pirates, called privateers, robbed only enemies of their country. They sailed under a letter of marque— permission from their king or queen.

Sea Queens

Some pirate ships flew black flags and some flew flags with beer mugs emblazoned on them.

Some pirates came from the upper classes.

Most pirates were hardworking sailors on the only ships that were democratically run by the crew instead of overseen by a tyrannical captain, the only ships with rules that favored the sailors.

And not all pirates were men.

Not all pirates were men?

Yes, some of the greatest pirates ever known were women. They usually dressed just like the men in loose trousers and full blouses. They fought like the men, too, with pistol and cutlass. But few on board were actually fooled into thinking they were men. Pirate ships were close quarters: the

Pirate Flags

The most popular pirate flag was the Jolly Roger. It consisted of a black background and, usually, a drawing of a skull-and-crossbones. The skull-and-crossbones was the symbol that captains drew in their ships' logs to show that a sailor had died. Sometimes the flag sported an hourglass, cutlass, bleeding heart, or dart. Some pirate flags were not black at all, but were red, which the pirates called "bloody."

sailors slept in the same rooms, used the same buckets of water for bathing, and when it came to bathroom facilities . . . well, that would have been hard to disguise.

Still, whether the pirates came from the lower classes or the upper, whether they did their pirating on the rivers or the high seas, and under whatever flag they flew, this much is true: they were all thieves and they often committed horrible deeds. They pillaged and murdered and sank many ships.

Even the women. Especially the women.

The Pirate Code

Pirate ships tended to be democratic societies in that they voted for their captains and they drew up their own rules, known as "articles." These articles were written out, and they outlined how the plunder would be divided, and how bad behavior would be punished. Each pirate had to make his mark or write his name on the paper and swear an oath to abide by the rules.

The pirates called themselves "honest men" and "gentlemen," though for the most part they came from the lowest ranks of society. Still, they spoke proudly of their "conscience" and "honor."

Pirates, Sailors, and Women

Like most sailors, pirates did not want women on board. Women were thought to bring bad luck to ships.

From pirate Bartholomew Roberts' article 3: That any man who "carried a woman off to sea disguised, he was to suffer death."

Sea Queens

Much of what we know about pirates does not come from the pirates themselves. Only a few kept journals. Most of them did not even know how to write. But there are trial documents, logbooks of navy captains, and depositions from captured pirates and their victims.

Remember, when most pirates lived, there were no cameras, no movies, no embedded reporters, and no recorders on the scene.

The woodcuts and engravings that decorate early books about pirates are probably as wildly inaccurate as the stories themselves.

Walking the plank. Think of Captain Hook and all the many other tales of this cruel rite. Then ask yourself—what pirates actually had time for such things? In the midst of battle, they simply hacked their enemies to death and flung the bodies over the ship's side. After the battle, they made sure to sail off quickly with their treasures, so they couldn't be captured themselves.

Treasures. Are you thinking chests of gold and pieces of eight? Are you thinking caskets of jewels and strands of pearls? More likely the treasure consisted of bales of cotton or silk, barrels of tobacco or apples, sails, extra rope, salt pork, rum, carpenter tools, goats, chickens—or slaves. And the enemy ship as well.

Remember Who They Were

"Cruel they undoubtedly were; and relatively few of them received the hempen halter they deserved. But their crimes should be remembered as taking place in a cruel age, when even children might be hanged for stealing less than a dollar's worth of goods. Nor should it be forgotten that most pirates had either fled from the widespread miseries of poverty . . . or had been recruited as deserters from the armies and navies of Europe."

—Robert I. Nesmith, foreword to *Pirates of the Spanish Main*

Reverend S. Baring-Gould collected several versions
of this ballad, which is sometimes sung as
"Female Pirate" or "The Female Buccaneer."

O come list a while, and you shall hear,
By the rolling sea lived a maiden fair.
Her father had followed the smuggling trade,
Like a warlike hero.
Like a warlike hero that never was afraid.

Now, in sailor's clothing young Jane did go,
Dressed like a sailor from top to toe.
Her aged father was the only care
Of this female smuggler.
Of this female smuggler who never did despair.

With her pistols loaded she went aboard.
And by her side hung a glittering sword,
In her belt two daggers; well armed for war
Was this female smuggler,
Was this female smuggler,
   who never feared a scar.

Now they had not sail-ed far from the land,
When a strange sail brought them to a stand.
"These are sea robbers," this maid did cry,
"But the female smuggler,
But the female smuggler will conquer
   or will die."

Alongside, then, this strange vessel came.
"Cheer up," cried Jane, "we will board the
   same;
We'll run all chances to rise or fall,"
Cried this female smuggler,
Cried this female smuggler,
   who never feared a ball.

Now they killed those pirates and
   took their store,
And soon returned to old Eng-a-land's shore.
With a keg of brandy she walked along,
Did this female smuggler,
Did this female smuggler,
   and sweetly sang a song.

Now they were followed by the blockade,
Who in irons strong did put this fair maid.
But when they brought her for to be te-ried,
This young female smuggler,
This young female smuggler stood
   dressed like a bride.

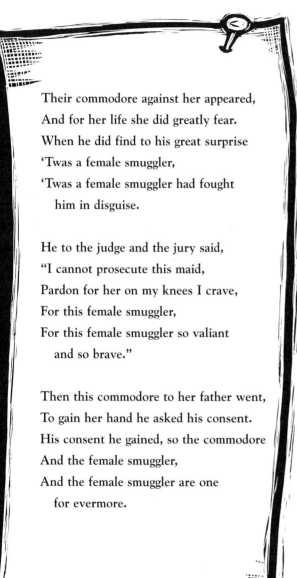

Their commodore against her appeared,
And for her life she did greatly fear.
When he did find to his great surprise
'Twas a female smuggler,
'Twas a female smuggler had fought
  him in disguise.

He to the judge and the jury said,
"I cannot prosecute this maid,
Pardon for her on my knees I crave,
For this female smuggler,
For this female smuggler so valiant
  and so brave."

Then this commodore to her father went,
To gain her hand he asked his consent.
His consent he gained, so the commodore
And the female smuggler,
And the female smuggler are one
  for evermore.

How Women Pirates Dressed

"In times when men and women wore very different kinds of garb, one could persuade others that he or she belonged to the other sex simply by changing his or her outfit. . . . This use of dress to fool the audience is the basis of the longstanding folklore of women dressing as men to go to sea."
—Joan Druett, *She Captains: Heroines and Hellions of the Sea*

Since most Western sailors wore their hair long, tied in a pigtail, and tarred, girls and women could pass easily. As for clothes, sailors usually wore baggy petticoat-breeches and a loose shirt under a jacket. The only time sailors removed their clothes in public was when a doctor undressed them to treat a wound.

Artemisia, Admiral-Queen

Persia: 500–480 BC

Named after Artemis, the Greek goddess of the hunt, Artemisia was queen of Halicarnassus, one of the Greek states on the west coast of what is now Turkey.

Artemisia had become queen by marrying the king of Halicarnassus in 500 BC. His name is lost to history. When he died a few years later, she became sole ruler. Though little is known about Artemisia, this is: she led her ships in action against other Greek city-states long before the main battle that would make her famous. In fact, she was successful enough in her pirate raids to become a military advisor to King Xerxes of Persia, the biggest superpower of the day.

Artemisia was a member of Xerxes' military council and the only advisor to speak against fighting the Greeks in a naval battle. Xerxes didn't listen to her advice and tried to smash the Greek fleet during the sea battle of Salamis, the first naval battle recorded in history, around September 20, 480 BC. Xerxes watched from a golden throne on the shore. Finding that she was trapped between the Greek ships and the Persian fleet, Artemisia rammed her ship, *Lykos*, into a Greek trireme (a galley with three banks of oars) that was blocking her exit, and so made her escape. Believing her to be an ally, the trireme did not pursue her ship. King Xerxes knew she'd hit the enemy ship. He is reputed to have said, "My men have become women, and my women have become men."

Legal Pirating

In ancient Greece and the surrounding countries, pirating was considered a craft.

By law these pirates were protected as an "association," something like a guild or union. Some pirates even dedicated a portion of their loot to the goddess Hera, who ruled the winds.

Artemisia

Although heavily outnumbered, the Greeks ended up winning what turned out to be one of the most important naval victories of all time.

After this battle Artemisia returned to pirating. She was so successful that the Athenians offered a prize of ten thousand drachma to anyone who captured her.

Who First Wrote About the Battle of Salamis?

Herodotus, an ancient Greek historian who lived in the fifth century BC, wrote a book called *The Histories*, which included the battle of Salamis. Herodotus wanted both to preserve the memory of the past as well as to show how Greeks and non-Greeks came into conflict.

The Athenian playwright Aeschylus, who was himself in the battle, wrote a play about it called *The Persians*.

What we know about the naval battle dates back to these two sources.

Queen Teuta

Illyria: circa 230 BC

King Agron established the first kingdom of Illyria with his second wife, Teuta. When he died of pneumonia after a banquet, Teuta was regent for her stepson Pinneus, who was too young to rule.

Her first royal decision was to give her ships the right to plunder up and down the coast. They brought home so much booty that Teuta was well pleased and sent them off again, this time southward into the Ionian Sea, then westward along the Italian coast. Each time they returned with treasure, Teuta rewarded them. She

Where is Illyria?

Modern-day Albanians are believed to have descended from the Illyrians, whose country extended from Dalmatia on the north to the Aoos (Vijose) River on the south.

The Illyrians were a group of many tribes living in the western part of the Balkans. That includes modern Slovenia in the northwest to halfway down the mainland of modern Greece.

also occasionally went with them on their raids. Soon she was known as the Terror of the Adriatic.

The Roman senate felt that this could not continue and sent ambassadors to demand an end to all piracy. But the piracy had proved too successful. Furthermore, according to Illyrian law, it was a legal trade. During the meeting one of the envoys was so disrespectful to Teuta she had him killed on his way home.

Now Rome could not back down. War was declared immediately, and in 229 BC Roman armies crossed the Adriatic for the first time ever. An enormous Roman fleet of two hundred ships forced Teuta's governor

Queen Teuta

Illyrian Boats

Teuta's boats were small, fast, single-banked galleys called *lembi*, according to Joan Druett in *She Captains*.

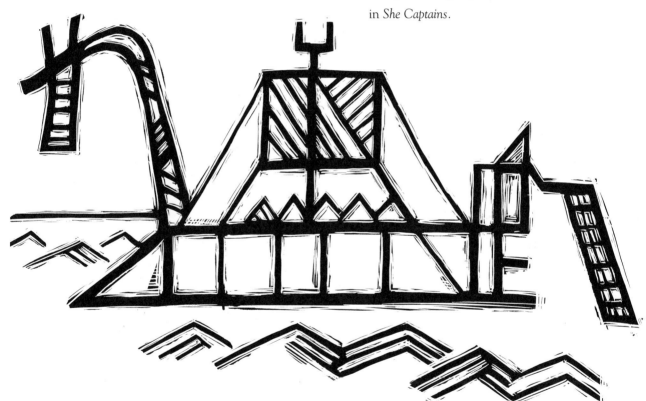

Demetrius to surrender. In return he was given a great part of her holdings. Together army and navy subdued one town after another, finally besieging the capital city.

In 227 BC Teuta surrendered. The Romans allowed her to remain regent, but her holdings were now tiny. Further, she was forbidden to sail any armed ship south of the capital. She also had to pay an annual tribute to Rome. Her reign as pirate queen of the Adriatic had lasted less than four years.

Was Teuta Real?

The Illyrians were illiterate, so much of what we know of these early times is in legends and stories passed down through the ages, mouth to ear. The Roman side of the story *was* written down. However, the remains of Teuta's palace and Demetrius's fortress are still visible near Sucuraj in Albania.

Teuta's Mistake

Teuta's first mistake was letting her ships prey on Roman ships. Her second mistake was to thumb her nose at Roman requests. Her third was to allow a Roman ambassador to be killed without consequences for those who killed him. Rome was the great power in the world at that time and till then had never tried to cross over into Illyria. Once Rome had an excuse to march into Illyria, it was only a matter of time before the country was subjugated.

Alfhild

Denmark: ninth century

Alfhild's Names

Alvilda
Alfhilda
Alvild
Alwilda the Danish
Female Pirate

Siward (or Synardus), king of the Goths, had a daughter Alfhild who was so modest that she kept her face muffled in her robe so that her beauty should not stun the men around her.

Wanting to keep his daughter safe, her father gave her a viper to raise so that it would be her guardian. Further, he warned that any man who came into her chamber would be beheaded and his dead body impaled on a stake.

Sea Queens

Now this sounds like any good old-fashioned fairy tale. But in fact during the Viking period men often tried to capture rich brides by stealing them away. Siward added this warning: should a prince get through to his daughter, she would only be wed if she wanted to—as the saga says, if she made "a free and decided choice."

Many princes tried and failed to win Alfhild. Then Alf, son of Sigar (or Sygardus), decided to try. What an imaginative wooer he turned out to be. First he covered his body "with a blood-stained hide," in part for protection and in part to get the viper all worked up. Then, when it attacked him, he held a pair of tongs that gripped a piece of "red-hot steel" and plunged it "into the yawning throat of the viper." Then he was ready to claim his prize.

But Alfhild did not want Alf as a husband. Perhaps she was angry that he'd murdered her pet. Perhaps she didn't like his manners. Whatever her reasons, she changed into men's clothing and went off on her own to

About Viking Longboats

Viking boats were between seventy and one hundred feet long, and double-ended. They were clinker-built, which meant their wooden planks overlapped for extra strength. For even more protection, the sailors hung their round shields over the side of the ship.

The ships were called *snigs*, *skeidhs*, or dragons. At the bow—the front of the ship— was a carved figurehead, usually some sort of dragon. Though there was a single bank of oars, these ships were meant for sailing. The sails were made by Viking women from bright silks, often embroidered with golden threads. In fact the entire boat was a work of art, with gilt-covered masts and red dye on the rigging.

Most important of all the Viking ships had a shallow draft, which meant they could sail up rivers where other boats could not go. Therefore they could sail within range of much of the countryside, so that even inland communities were not safe from the raiders.

become a sea rover, or viking, a warrior on the sea. As Olaus Magnus wrote, "she began to reject all men and firmly resolved . . . to surpass male courage in the practice of piracy."

Alfhild recruited a crew of women and soon they found a boat. The saga reported that the women "happened to come to a spot where a band of rovers were lamenting the death of their captain," and they were so taken with Alfhild's beauty that they presented her with the command. Or perhaps she found a boat unguarded and simply took what she wanted. Danish law at the time declared, "Seafarers may use what gear they find, including boat or tackle."

And so Alfhild began her career as a sea rover. She did so well that by the end of the saga she commanded a full fleet. She preyed on so many ships in the Baltic, and on Danish soil as well, that the Danish king sent out fleets of his own to stop her.

Prince Alf was sent on her trail. He made "many toilsome voyages in pursuit of her."

Alfhild

About Alfhild's Tale

Scandinavian bards, called *skalds*, sang great epic stories at the king's feast hall. *"Hwaet!"* they would say loudly, "Listen!" And suddenly the tumult in the king's hall stilled because everyone loved a good tale. Sometimes the stories were old traditional sagas, sometimes tribal histories. Sometimes they were tales in which the king, in whose hall the story was told, featured as hero.

The oldest written version of the Alfhild saga comes from the twelfth century and was set down in Latin by Saxo Grammaticus in a sixteen-volume book, *Gesta Danorum* (Deeds of the Danes). Four hundred years later, in 1555, Alfhild's story was retold by Olaf the Great in *Historia de Gentibus Septentrionalibus* (History of the Northern Peoples).

Another three centuries on, the Boston writer Charles Ellms rewrote Alfhild's tale—making lots of mistakes—in his 1837 *The Pirates Own Book: Authentic Narratives of the Most Celebrated Sea Robbers.*

Most Scandinavian medieval history was oral, although rune stones on which inscriptions were scratched in the old Norse language were used primarily to mark deaths and public events in the early Middle Ages.

And finally he found her, in the narrow Gulf of Finland. She attacked, and he managed to seize one after another of Alfhild's ships. Boarding her flagship at last, Alf slaughtered "all who withstood him." And then his lieutenant, Borgar, struck off Alfhild's helmet.

Her beauty stopped Alf in his tracks and instead of fighting her, he kissed her and made her his wife. They ruled Denmark and had a daughter, Gurid.

Is it true?

Well, there were reports of other women of that time taking to the sea. Queen Aud, widow of the king of Dublin, led a navy to Iceland. In *The Anglo-Saxon Chronicles*, Aedelflaed was known as a brilliant commander in both sea and land battles against the Danes. So—possible? Yes. But certainly not true in all parts.

Alfhild Artifacts

At Mystic Seaport in Connecticut are two pieces of walrus tusk scrimshaw incised with Alfhild's image. However, instead of being clothed in a fifth-century Viking warrior outfit, she is wearing what looks like a Turkish costume, trousers with a full-skirted coat. She carries a curved cutlass, and a pistol is stuck in her belt. Neither of these is the right period or country of origin for Alfhild.

Why is Alfhild on these scrimshaws? Probably some enterprising sailor, having heard the story, thought he could sell the scrimshaw for an inflated price when he got home, claiming it was an original drawing from the ninth century. Only a scholar would know the difference.

Jeanne de Belleville

Brittany: fourteenth century

From the stories surrounding Brittany's long fight for independence comes the tale of Jeanne de Belleville, known as The Lioness of Brittany.

The date was 1343 when Jeanne de Belleville, a noblewoman, began her pirating career. Before this she had lived quietly with her husband, Olivier de Clisson, and their two sons in a fine house in the countryside. They had friends at court and moved in the highest circles.

This was a time of war—England against France.

Jeanne's Names

There are three women—or rather three names—associated with this (hi)story: Jeanne de Montford, Jeanne de Belleville, and Jeanne de Clisson. It is possible that one is our Jeanne's maiden name and one her place of birth.

27

Sea Queens

France against England. And Brittany against everyone. Some unknown person in the French court accused Olivier of siding with the English. He had no way to clear his name and was quickly imprisoned, then executed. His head was sent from Paris to Nantes, where it was displayed on the city wall.

Jeanne was devastated, both at her husband's death and the manner of it. However, instead of sitting around and weeping, she vowed revenge. She sold her castles, lands, and jewels. With the money, she manned and equipped three large ships. Then, taking her teenage sons with her, she set out to exact that revenge.

Cruising the coast of Normandy, she attacked French vessels, killing everyone aboard. She ravaged the French

Where Is Brittany?

Brittany juts defiantly out into the Atlantic from the upper northwest corner of France. It has a wonderful long, jagged coastline.

The Bretons, who lived in Great Britain, were driven out by the Anglo-Saxons to Brittany around AD 500. They were such successful colonizers that their name was given to the people there.

Brittany's history is one of a long struggle for independence. First the Bretons tried to get rid of their Frank overlords (fifth to ninth centuries), then they tried to rid themselves of the dukes of Normandy and the counts of Anjou (tenth to twelfth centuries), and afterwards they fought against both England and France. In 1532 Brittany was finally made a part of France.

countryside. It was said Jeanne de Belleville could often be seen, sword in one hand, torch in the other, standing in the ruins of a Normandy village.

In 1345 she supported the English invasion of Brittany in the hopes of ridding her country of the French influence. No one knows what happened to her after that.

Grania O'Malley

Ireland: sixteenth century

Gray-eyed, dark-haired Grania O'Malley was born in Connacht on the west coast of Ireland around 1530.

Her father was the clan chieftain Dudara "Black Oak" O'Malley, a famous sea captain widely known to be "strong in galleys and seamen." Her mother was a noblewoman, Margaret O'Malley. Grania was their only daughter.

The O'Malleys were seafarers; their family motto was *Terra Marique Potems*—"Powerful by Land and

Sea Queens

Sea." But at that time the O'Malleys could not trade in salt fish at their nearest port, Galway, for it was in English hands.

Dudara was not happy with this situation, so he led his followers to Scotland, France, and Spain to trade, which did not make him popular with the English king, Henry VIII, nor later with his daughter, Queen Elizabeth I. Nor was the king of Spain pleased with him because Black Oak O'Malley forced foreign ships (that is, non-Irish ships) to pay a toll to fish in Irish waters. In 1556 alone King Philip of Spain had to pay the O'Malleys one thousand pounds (an enormous sum for that time) for twenty-one years of fishing rights.

Grania went along on many of these trading trips. With her hair cut short—almost unheard-of for girls of her day—she looked like a boy. One day when returning from a trading trip to Spain, Dudara's ship was attacked by the English. Grania was ordered to safety below, but she refused. Bravely she watched the fight, and even more bravely leaped onto the back of one man who was attacking her father. This saved her father and the day.

At age fifteen Grania was married to Donal-an-Cogahaidh O'Flaherty (Donal of the Battles). The two hardly knew one another, but the marriage was more the alliance of two great Irish families than a love match. Besides, the O'Flahertys were known to be so fierce that people in the Galway churches regularly prayed, "From the ferocious O'Flahertys, the Good Lord deliver us."

Grania and Donal had two sons, Owen and Murrough, and a daughter. But Donal was not a good or popular leader. He often got into trouble with rival clans. It

Women in Old Ireland

Under Irish law women were allowed more freedom than their English counterparts. They could choose their own husbands with their parents' approval, and they could divorce them anytime they wanted. They could own their own property, and if they brought money into marriage, they could decide to pay their men's debts or not, while Englishwomen's money and property belonged to their husbands.

was said of him that he killed his own stepnephew. Whether or not that charge was true, his clanspeople led miserable lives. Many ended up starving during Donal's embattled rule.

Donal was killed fighting against one of those rival clans, in his stronghold known as Cock's Castle. Grania took over, leading the men in a massive defeat of their enemy. The castle was immediately renamed Hen's Castle by her delighted army.

Grania's Daughter

The name of Grania's daughter has been lost to history, but she was married off to a neighboring chief of Corraun, Richard "Devil's Hook" Gurke. In this way Grania strengthened her position along the coast.

Now Grania had authority with the fighters, but Irish law would not let her inherit her husband's title. So she recruited two hundred of the best fighting men and went back to her father's territory, basing her operations on Clare Island. There she began to control all the shipping along the coast by charging for protection and hiring out navigators. When those ploys failed, she took to pirating, raiding any ships that would not pay. Her boats each had one hundred men aboard and were rowed with thirty oars when not under sail. The sailors knew the bays and coastline of Connaught so well that in little time they had built up a fortune for Grania.

Since Ireland was such a poor nation, and England kept her poorer still, soon the peasants were lining up to work for Grania, even those whose clans were at war with one another. Grania expanded her fleet with captured ships.

Then in 1566 Grania wed for a second time, to Richard-an-Iarainn (Richard in Iron) Burke. He was so called because he always wore a coat of mail. Again Grania married for alliance's sake, to gain Rockfleet Castle and all of Clew Bay, which was under Burke's control.

Now in those days the Irish legal system provided that there could be an easy divorce by either husband or wife if it occurred during the first year. At the end of a year, Grania divorced Richard in Iron. It is

The Burkes

The Burkes were as important a clan as the O'Malleys, the family descended from the famous king Charlemagne.

One of Richard's ancestors was supposedly the great Irish hero-king Brian Boru. The English said Richard was "a plundering, warlike, unquiet, rebellious man," which should have made him a perfect match for Grania.

said that she simply locked him out of the castle, and shouted down the stairs, "I dismiss you."

Oddly, though, Grania and Richard must have been in love, for they remained together—though divorced—until Richard died seventeen years later.

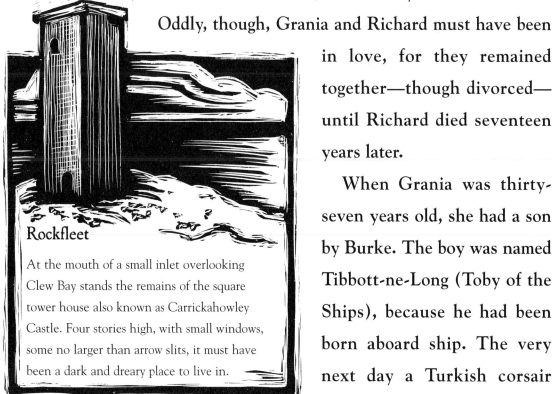

Rockfleet

At the mouth of a small inlet overlooking Clew Bay stands the remains of the square tower house also known as Carrickahowley Castle. Four stories high, with small windows, some no larger than arrow slits, it must have been a dark and dreary place to live in.

When Grania was thirty-seven years old, she had a son by Burke. The boy was named Tibbott-ne-Long (Toby of the Ships), because he had been born aboard ship. The very next day a Turkish corsair attacked Grania's ship. Things were going so badly that the sailors came racing to her cabin to ask for her help. She climbed out of bed, handed the baby to a nurse, cursed the sailors for being so helpless, threw a blanket over her shoulders, grabbed up two blunderbusses, and went out on deck. There

Grania O'Malley

she fired off her pistols at the leaders of the Turkish ship and led her men to victory.

Grania was now such a powerful force along the coast that the English decided they had to stop her.

Grania's Boats

They were galleys, as described in 1601 by Captain Plessington of HMS *Tremontaney*, "rowed with thirty oars, and had on board, ready to defend her, one hundred good shot, which entertained skirmish with my boat at most an hour."

Sea Queens

They lay siege to Rockfleet Castle in 1574. But she led her men on an attack, forcing the English to flee.

However, the English would not give up. Three years later, in order to keep them from her shores, Grania was forced to pledge loyalty to Queen Elizabeth, just three years her junior. In exchange Richard was made a knight and Grania was called Lady Burke. It is said that for once Grania put on female clothes for the ceremony.

Did this stop her from raiding ships? Not at all. However, in 1577 she was captured by the English and put in prison in Dublin Castle for a year and a half. She managed to convince her jailers that she would betray her husband, who was busy with an uprising of his own, and so they let her go. But instead Grania

What Some Famous People of Her Time Said of Grania O'Malley

"A most famous feminine sea captain . . . famous for her stoutness of courage, and person and for sundry other exploits done by her at sea."—Sir Henry Sidney

"A woman that hath . . . been a great spoiler, and chief commander and director of thieves and murderers at sea to spoil this province." —Lord Justice William Drury

"The nurse of all rebellions in Connaught for the last forty years!"—Sir Richard Bingham

raced back to Rockfleet and joined Richard, and they lived together for another five years before he died of natural causes.

The new English governor of Connaught, Sir Richard Bingham, decided that this was the time to bring all of his area under strict control. In 1586 he captured Grania and her men, stole their possessions, and built a gallows on which to hang them. Grania was prepared to die, but instead her son-in-law, known as Devil's Hook, took her place as a hostage. Sadly, though, Grania also saw her oldest son Owen brutally murdered, stabbed twelve times.

Grania's Exploits

Grania did not just pirate ships on the sea. She was also responsible for saving the lives of many English Protestants who were being prosecuted during Queen Mary's (or Bloody Mary's) rule.

Her men were loyal to her because she was careful to take good care of them and their families.

In 1592 the hated Bingham raided Grania's pirate haven as well and seized all of the fleet that was anchored in Clew Bay. Fleeing to Ulster, Grania was able to organize a rebellion and bring both Irish and Scots to her cause.

Sea Queens

Pirate or Privateer?

A pirate is a robber on the sea. During the time of King Henry VII in Britain (16th century) a law was passed that made illegal all robbery and murder along any river, creek, estuary, or place where the lord high admiral had jurisdiction.

A privateer is a licensed pirate, allowed by law to attack and seize ships of the king's (or queen's) enemies. The monarch issued a letter of marque, which was nothing more than a certificate that gave permission for this legal piracy. The captain kept a journal of everything taken in battle, and a portion of his booty had to be sent to the royal coffers. It was a cheap way for a ruler to run a navy.

Grania now realized that if she were to salvage something from this constant warfare, she had to do it queen to queen. So in July 1593, at age sixty-three, she wrote to Queen Elizabeth: from "your loyal and faithful subject Granny Ne Mailly of Connaught in your Highness realm of Ireland." She offered to put her men and ships in the queen's cause if Elizabeth would "grant her some reasonable maintenance for the little time she has to live."

Elizabeth obviously liked this feisty woman. She wrote back with a list of eighteen questions. Grania answered them carefully and asked for a face-to-face meeting. Astonishingly the meeting was granted, and Grania sailed off to Greenwich in September.

No one knows what the two of them spoke about, except that they conversed in Latin. But Grania must have been persuasive. The result was that the queen granted Grania a pension, and Tibbot-ne-Long, who had been arrested, was set free.

Grania sailed back to Connaught, having been given permission from the queen to "pursue, during her life,

A Legend About Meeting Queen Elizabeth

Grania wore a yellow skirt and yellow girdle with a green cape of the clan chiefs draped over her shoulders. At one point she sneezed in the royal presence. Alarmed, a courtier gave her a silken handkerchief. She blew her nose in it, then tossed it in a nearby fireplace. Everyone at court was shocked, but Grania said, "Back home we get rid of these disgusting things." It is said that the queen laughed.

all Her Majesty's enemies by land and sea." It was a license for privateering.

Bingham was appalled and tried to stop Grania, calling her a "traitoress," and placing guards around her. But he could not go against the queen's orders. Two years later Bingham himself was removed from his office in disgrace.

But Grania was growing old and tired. She put her son Tibbot in charge of her fleet. He was eventually given the title of Viscount Mayo.

Grania lived on until 1603, dying at seventy-three in the same year that Queen Elizabeth died. No other pirate queen has ruled as long.

Grania O'Malley

A Legend About Sailing Home

Returning from her meeting with the queen, Grania sailed up to Howth Castle looking for a place to spend the night. In those days Irish hospitality meant that any stranger was entitled to a meal and a bed. But when she got to the castle she was turned away, told that the lord of Howth was eating and couldn't be disturbed.

Furious, Grania left, and as she was returning to her boat she met a maidservant with a young, well-dressed boy in tow, the son of the castle's lord. She grabbed the boy, sailed off, and sent back a ransom note with the nurse. The lord of Howth Castle promised Grania anything she wanted for the return of his son. What she asked for was that from that day forth, the gates at Howth Castle would ever be open, and that anyone who asked always be entitled to a meal and a place to stay for the night. It is said that today the family that owns Howth still sets an extra place at dinner in case an uninvited guest turns up.

Lady Killigrew

England: late sixteenth century

Sir John Killigrew was a man of high regard in the sixteenth century: a government official; vice admiral of Cornwall, an English county; and the head of the Cornwall Commission on Piracy. Ironically, however, his family had made a fortune through piracy and smuggling. His grandfather Philip Wolverston had been known as "the gentleman pirate of Suffolk." His uncle Peter robbed ships on the Irish Sea. Killigrew

Pendennis Castle

Pendennis Castle is over four hundred fifty years old. Built by Henry VIII, it began with a simple round tower and gate enclosed by a lower curtain wall. But during his daughter Elizabeth's reign, an extra wall was put up, encircling the structure. Today the castle has a Discovery Centre for visitors that explores the history of the castle and includes information about the Killigrews.

cousins John Michell and John Penrose were also in the pirate business. But perhaps most infamous was his mother, Lady Mary, who ran the family pirate business from Pendennis Castle, at the entrance to Falmouth Harbor.

Falmouth Harbor

In Britain's southwest corner lies the port of Falmouth Harbor, known as the world's third largest natural harbor, a gateway to a beautiful network of rivers and creeks.

It is famous for its beaches and castle but even more famous for its smugglers, wreckers, and pirates.

Though they had stopped ships and stolen cargo for years, the Killigrews were always careful not to pirate Queen Elizabeth I's ships, so they stayed out of trouble.

However, there came a night—in December 1582—when Lady Killigrew personally oversaw the taking of the wrong cargo as a prize. The *Marie de San Sebastien*, a well-built Spanish merchant ship, came into Falmouth Harbor after being battered by a hurricane. It was rumored to carry silks, spices, and barrels of Spanish doubloons.

With two trusted house servants—Henry Kendall and John Hawkins—as well as seven Flemish sailors, Lady Killigrew rowed out and attacked the ship, murdering the entire crew. Then she sent the Flemish sailors off with the boat, to sell it in a foreign port.

But Lady Mary's plans went awry because the owners, Juan de Chavis and Captain Philip de Oryo, were not aboard, having spent the night in the town of Penryn. Further, the stolen barrels contained only leather, some Holland cloth, and a few pieces of eight.

Arwenack House

The Killigrew family acquired the estate by marriage in 1403 and lived there for almost sixteen generations. They rebuilt the house in 1567, just a scant fifteen years before Lady Mary's terrible deed. Once described as "the finest and most costly house in the country," Arwenack House was destroyed by fire around 1646.

Chavis and Oryo took the case to the Commission on Piracy—where Sir John Killigrew sat as president. He recognized the Holland cloth and chairs as things that had recently appeared at his mother's house, Arwenack, as well as in his daughter's home.

Suspicion immediately fell on Kendall and Hawkins, but they both had alibis, so the commission brought back the following verdict: piracy by person or persons unknown.

However, suspecting the commission, Chavis and Oryo applied for safe conduct to London. Thinking the two were leaving for good, the commission let them go. But the Spaniards had a friend in court, the Earl of Bedford, a member of the Queen's Privy Council. It was an opportunity for the queen to break the power of the notorious Cornwall pirate syndicate.

Then in London, Kendall and Hawkins' alibi was shown to be false. Sir John's daughter Mary admitted receiving Holland cloth and two leather chairs from her grandmother on New Year's Day. The mystery was quickly solved.

Though Lady Mary was freed through influential

Pirate Syndicates

In the sixteenth century, piracy was a family business. A pirate ship needed a "safe harbor," a place where it could dock and its crew not be arrested. Falmouth Harbor was one of these safe harbors. Once there, a pirate captain would report to the syndicate leader with a list of his booty. The booty would be sold through the syndicate, which would take a share. Some pirate ships were even outfitted and manned by the syndicate. Poor country folk in Cornwall also rented out coves to pirate ships. In fact, everyone seemed to benefit—except, of course, the ships that had been robbed and the crews who had been killed.

friends, Kendall and Hawkins were sent to the gallows. Before they died, Kendall is reported to have said, "I lament nothing more than that we have not the company of that old Jesabel Killigrew at this place as in justice we ought to."

Lady Mary was forced to live in exile for the rest of her life. Sixteen years later Sir John was arrested and imprisoned for trying to help the Spanish invade England by renting them Falmouth Harbor. It was the end of the Killigrew pirate syndicate.

Pretty Peg and the Dutch Privateer

Holland: seventeenth century

At thirty, Henrik Van Dank, son of a Dutch trader, inherited his father's prosperous fleet. Because Holland was at war with England, he outfitted three of the ships as privateers: the flagship *Black Cutter*, plus the *Black Eagle* and the *Fury*.

However, no sooner were the ships a few miles to sea than the men mutinied, led by a man called Bold

Sea Queens

Dulken, a gunner on the *Eagle*. He sank the flagship and raced away. Left with only the *Fury*, Van Dank and a few loyal men limped back to port for repairs.

Van Dank's wife, Peg, was an Englishwoman, taller than her husband and hardier. She advised him to pick a new crew, and this time she would sail with him. She was a better sailor than he, and tougher, too. In no time they captured several English ships and much booty.

One day the *Fury* came upon Dulken and the stolen *Eagle*. Dulken managed to board Van Dank's ship with a small number of hand-picked men. It was decided that the two captains would fight in single combat with swords. Dulken drew first blood, and Van Dank went down on his knees. Just then Peg broke through the crowd of men, grabbed Dulken by his waist, and flung him overboard.

Holland Wars

Throughout the seventeenth century Holland was frequently at war with England. Privateers were outfitted and backed by merchants, bankers, and the upper classes, who were determined to keep the oceans open for their own purposes.

Holland in the 1690s was the most important Protestant power, despite its small size. A center for the arts and sciences and a gathering place for any victims of Catholic persecution, Holland was also at the heart of the financial world.

Then she picked up Dulken's sword and handed it to her husband.

The couple sailed for four more years together, when tragedy suddenly struck.

While leading a boarding party onto an English ship, Peg was shot dead by a young lieutenant. The pirates brought her body back to Van Dank. He laid it on the deck, and then he scuttled the *Fury*. His men swam for the safety of the English ship, but Van Dank went down with his boat. Life without his Pretty Peg was unthinkable.

The Sea Beggars

The Dutch privateers began in the 1560s, when William I, the Silent, the Prince of Orange, chartered the *Gueux de la Mer* (Beggars of the Sea) specifically to harass Spanish shipping. The men he gathered were adventurers, pirates, and those fighting against Spanish rule in the Dutch provinces.

The prince issued letters of marque authorizing the sailors to become privateers, and he gave these orders: "All Sea beggars to conform to the Articles of War; Each commander maintain a protestant minister on board his ship; All prizes to be divided and distributed by rule; Command functions must be by native Dutchmen unless expressly commissioned by the Prince Van Oranje; No persons on board, either as sailors or soldiers, save folk of good name and fame."

Charlotte de Berry

England: mid-seventeenth century

Though her name sounds French, Charlotte de Berry was born in England in 1636. Or perhaps she never lived at all. There is a great deal of controversy about her.

It is said she grew up dreaming of a life on the sea. After falling in love with a sailor, she married him and—disguised as a man—followed him when he was conscripted by the Royal Navy. They told everyone

55

they were brothers. But an officer accused Charlotte's husband of mutiny. The young sailor was found guilty and flogged so severely that he died. Charlotte killed the officer and fled.

Running off to London, she became an entertainer in waterfront saloons. There an ardent captain kidnapped her, forced her into marriage, and then set sail for Africa. Some say she cut off his head with a dagger and convinced the ship's crew to become pirates.

Another version of the story holds that the navy ship departed England, but pirates attacked it and killed Charlotte's new husband. The cruel pirate captain discovered Charlotte's identity, but she fought a duel with him and lopped off his head. The pirates

Truth or Fiction?

The earliest reference to Charlotte de Berry comes from Edward Lloyd's 1836 *History of the Pirates*, a book of gory stories in a format called "the penny dreadful" because it sold for a penny. They were the comic books of the day, sold to the masses.

In every print version of Charlotte's life since then, the story is pretty clearly a retelling of the 1836 tale. There is in fact no evidence of a Captain Rodolph at the time, though perhaps a pirate's name might not be written down in naval records.

The drawing of lots to decide who will be eaten comes right out of the much-reported 1820 ramming of the whale ship *Essex*. The story of that ill-fated voyage was published in 1821 by first mate Owen Chase. So perhaps Charlotte's entire story was invented for Lloyd's book.

made Charlotte their new captain. Dressed as a man, she called herself Captain Rodolph.

Supposedly after this she married her third husband, a wealthy Spaniard planter, who joined her crew. Three years later the ship sank in a storm. The survivors lasted eight days on a raft without food or water. At last they decided to draw lots. The loser would die and be eaten by the others. Sadly her husband was the first slain, just before a ship rescued them. Then pirates attacked the rescue ship, and Charlotte helped fight them off. She saved her rescuers, afterward leaping overboard to join her dead husband.

Anne Bonney and Mary Read

American colonies: early eighteenth century

The story of the most famous women pirates began in Ireland's County Cork around 1697 when a handsome lawyer fell in love with a serving girl, who gave birth to a daughter, Anne. The lawyer tried to pass the child off as a boy he was raising to be a clerk, but his wife discovered his deception and cut him out of an

Sea Queens

allowance. So he left her—eloping with the serving girl and their baby—to Canada and from there to the Carolinas, where he became a planter.

It was a hard life at first, and the Irishwoman died when Anne was still a baby. Without a mother she grew up headstrong and out of control, for her father didn't discipline her. In fact it was said she nearly killed a young man who made advances and stabbed the cook over an argument about a chicken dinner. Her father shrugged the stabbing off, saying that the cook "was in her time a pretty good cook, but she was a bit opinionated and my daughter is to be excused for losing her temper with her."

One of Anne's many boyfriends was James Bonney, a common sailor who'd been a pirate. He courted Anne as much for her inheritance as her beauty. Her

Piracy in the Carolinas

The Carolinas were a notorious haven for pirates in the 1700s. Pirates such as Charles Vane, Blackbeard, and Stede Bonnet terrorized the waters for years.

What made the Carolinas good for piracy? The shallow coastline, which was difficult for merchant ships and men-of-war, provided the perfect refuge for the smaller, shallow-draft pirate ships. Once they had their booty, the pirates could disappear with ease.

Also, a number of the governors had their hands out for bribes. The one most willing to allow the pirates free reign was Charles Eden, who not only pardoned Blackbeard and Bonnet in exchange for a handsome sum of money, but also allowed pirates to sell their goods at the local markets.

60

father warned that he would disinherit her if she married Bonney. Anne paid him no mind and eloped. True to his word, her father wrote her out of his will.

Broke, the newlyweds moved to Charles Town (now Nassau) on New Providence Island in the Bahamas, where Anne hoped they would join a pirate crew. But Bonney thought spying on his ex-comrades an easier way to turn a profit. He began informing Governor Woods Rogers in exchange for a pardon, which disgusted Anne. She started going out at night alone to visit the local taverns.

Anne's Poem

This poem is said to have been written by Anne Bonney:

Drain, drain, the bowl, each fearless soul—
Let the world wag as it will.
Let the heavens growl, the devil howl—
Drain, drain the bowl and fill!

In one tavern Anne met Calico Jack Rackham, quartermaster of Charles Vane's pirate ship. Jack offered Bonney money to let him have Anne as a wife. When that didn't work, Anne and Jack decided to run off. Getting wind of their plan, Bonney asked the governor's soldiers to catch Anne and bring her back, with the warning that should she run away again, she'd get a public whipping.

But that sort of warning hadn't worked on Anne before. Dressed in a pair of Calico Jack's striped seamen's trousers, a cutlass by her side, and two pistols in her belt, she sneaked out to meet Rackham and eight of his men at the waterfront. There they renamed her Tom Bonney and rowed out to a handsome sloop, the *Vanity*. It was said to be the fastest boat in the islands.

Climbing over the side of the ship, Jack, Anne, and their men overpowered the anchor watch and chained them below. Then Jack cut the cables and off they sailed, first setting the anchor watch ashore. With Rackham as captain and George Fetherston as quartermaster, they began their pirate careers.

The men knew that Tom Bonney was a woman and

How Anne's Story Was Told

From the first, Anne's story was embroidered by retellers. Some of the earliest anecdotes were put down in 1724 in *A General History of the Robberies and Murders of the Most Notorious Pyrates* by Captain Charles Johnson. It is probably as much fiction as fact. Many scholars believe the book was actually written by the novelist Daniel Defoe, author of *Robinson Crusoe*.

Rackham's common-law wife, but she was treated no differently than any of the men. However, when she became pregnant, she had Jack set her ashore in Cuba for the final months so as not to be in the way. Two months later, leaving the baby on shore with a nurse, Anne (Tom) Bonney returned to the *Vanity*. (Some accounts say the baby actually died.)

By then the pirates were "at low game"—not doing well because of having such a small crew—so Rackham hired on more hands. One of these was a tall, handsome sailor named James Morris.

Mary Read's story began quite differently. Her father was a captain of an English trading ship. His mother had promised him and his wife a sizeable fortune should they have a son.

How American Pirates Attacked

A common method of attack was made from the stern (the back) of the boat. The ship would maneuver alongside its victim. Four or five of the strongest men threw out grapnel hooks that caught the side of the other boat, then pulled their own boat as close as possible. Next they leaped onto the deck of the victim ship. Armed with large wooden mallets, two other pirates drove wedges of wood between the rudder and sternpost so the victim's ship could not get away.

Sea Queens

Their first baby was a boy, but he died very young. Then, with her husband away at sea, the captain's wife found she was pregnant again, this time giving birth to a girl. When her husband died at sea, she dressed Mary as a boy to fool her rich mother-in-law, who "allowed a Crown a Week for its Maintenance." But when the old woman died, she left them not a penny more.

It's said that Mary became set in her masculine ways from an early age. Her mother apprenticed her to a lady as a footboy known as Buttons. It was such a dull job—blacking boots and running errands—that Mary ran off to sea. She became a powder monkey, a boy who carries explosives from the magazine to the guns on board a warship.

She hated the discipline, and when the ship was in an English port, she deserted and ran off to Flanders to enlist as a soldier. There she "carry'd Arms in a Regiment of Foot, as a Cadet."

Soon tired of all the marching, Mary ran off to join the cavalry. There she fell in love with a fellow soldier,

Women as Soldiers

There are many stories of women disguising themselves as boys and running off to the army. One of the most famous was Deborah Samson of Plympton, Massachusetts, who called herself Robert Shurtliff and in 1778 joined the American army to fight against the British in the American War for Independence.

She served for three years and was wounded twice. The first time she received a sword cut to the side of the head, and later she was shot through the shoulder. Neither of these wounds exposed her as a woman. But when she came down with a "brain fever," the attending physician, Dr. Binney, discovered she was female. He took her to his own home to give her better care, and when she was well again he revealed her secret to her commanding officer, who kept her out of harm's way after that.

her tent mate, following him around till the entire regiment noticed. After Mary revealed to him that she was really a woman—which surprised him greatly—he returned her love and they were quickly married. They left the army and, with the help of monies from the officers, set up an inn near Breda Castle and the army garrison. The inn was called the "Sign of the Three Horseshoes."

The inn did well and officers dined regularly at its tables. But first Mary's husband died of a fever, and then the Peace of Utrecht was signed in 1713. The garrison was closed and officers no longer ate at the inn.

Putting on men's clothes once more, Mary ran off to sea on a Dutch ship bound for the West Indies. Not far from shore, English pirates captured the ship. Given the choice between being put in a small open boat on the sea or joining the pirates, Mary chose piracy. By the time they reached the New World, the pirates were quite rich and went their separate ways.

But Mary now had a taste for piracy. It suited her well. So she planned to go on to New Providence, where she hoped to join the Woods Rogers' privateers. As a privateer, she could keep having the exciting adventures of a pirate but be protected by the law. Still, when two weeks later the men on her new ship voted to become pirates, Mary went along with them. In one of their raids, a quiet sailor was brought on board. Mary fell in love again.

The quartermaster, though, took exception to the quiet man and insulted him. A duel was arranged.

Afraid her man would lose, and knowing herself to be a better shot, Mary picked a fight with the quartermaster and set the time of her duel for an earlier hour.

The duelists went off to a nearby island before dawn. At twenty paces they turned and fired. The quartermaster missed, but Mary's shot hit the mark. She walked over to him, bared her breast, and said, "You called me a woman and struck me on the cheek. Well! It is in truth a woman who kills you that she may teach others to respect her." It was her seventeenth duel.

By the time they reached port, Mary disclosed her secret to the quiet sailor. They were married on shore. But as the man she'd killed had been a favorite of the captain's, Mary and her husband decided it would be safer to ship with Calico Jack Rackham and his crew. It was 1720, and Mary joined the crew as James Morris.

Who was Woods Rogers?

In the West Indies by the mid-1660s, the waters around the islands were often besieged by pirates who found haven in the small coves. Since the pirates often raided Spanish ships, Spain sent its navy in 1695 to invade and destroy Charles Town on the island of New Providence.

The city was rebuilt and named Nassau. Twenty years later King George I appointed Captain Woods Rogers as the first royal governor of the Bahamas. Rogers was an ex-pirate himself and knew all the tricks, which made him an excellent choice for the job.

Sea Queens

Was this Anne Bonney's first meeting with a woman she could admire?

Were they both disguised at first in men's clothing? When did Anne know Mary was female? These are all questions history does not answer.

However, Captain Charles Johnson's account, though highly fictionalized, makes it clear that they became fast friends and that Rackham suspected the tall, handsome sailor had stolen his wife's heart. So Mary disclosed herself to him as well, which made matters easier on the small ship.

Just as well, since 1720 started out as a bad year for the *Vanity's* crew. They captured several fishing boats and raided some cattle farms on Haiti. They sacked two small sloops near Jamaica. They stole a twelve-ton sloop, *William*, in Nassau Harbor.

Finally on October 17, near Port Maria Bay on Jamaica's north coast, they found a great prize. It was a schooner belonging to Captain James Spenlow. The pirates' take was fifty rolls of tobacco, nine bags of

Anne Bonney and Mary Read

Who Knew They Were Women?

Rackham's sloop was small, and disguise would have been hard. It was clear to everyone that Anne was female. After all, she was the captain's common-law wife.

It has been pointed out that some of their victims knew Anne and Mary were women. One eyewitness, Dorothy Thomas, who had been in a canoe that was attacked by the pirates, declared that the women "wore Men's jackets, and long Trouzers, and Handkerchiefs tied about their heads" but that she knew they were women "by the largeness of their Breasts."

Two captured Frenchmen swore at their trial that at most times the two women wore "Women's Cloaths," though when they got ready for battle they put on men's gear.

Both quotes come from the transcript of the trial, which was printed in Jamaica by Robert Baldwin in 1721.

Then how much is true about their disguises, and how much is fiction? Were they both in their twenties, or was Mary much older? If he were still alive, we could ask Captain Johnson, a.k.a. Daniel Defoe. But alas, that avenue is closed to us now.

pimentos, and the ship's rigging. It was their biggest haul of the year—and their biggest mistake. Spenlow had already been robbed once that year, and so when he was released he went right to Governor Woods Rogers and gave a minute description of Rackham's ship and crew.

Governor Rogers sent Captain Jonathan Barnet on a man-of-war, *Albion*, with forty-five men, to accompany a Cuba-bound merchant ship through the same waters where Spenlow's ship had just been robbed. The two ships rounded the westernmost point of Jamaica and spotted Rackham's sloop.

Quietly the *Albion* slipped through the waves, but when they got close, Barnet saw only two men on deck. What he didn't know, though, was that the two were Anne and Mary. The rest of the crew were below, drinking stolen rum with nine turtle fisherman.

The women called down the hatch for help, and when the men refused, Anne fired a blast down, killing

Captain Barnet's Attack

Barnet's first broadside took out the *William*'s boom, which left the sloop dead in the water. He followed with a volley of small shot. So it was easy to then board the pirate ship. The sailors were met by Anne and Mary who were armed with cutlasses and pistols and shouting curses.

Barnet was known as "a brisk fellow," and so he proved in the battle with Rackham's ship.

one pirate and injuring several others. Then, shoulder to shoulder, she and Mary prepared to battle the man-of-war. But of course the women were quickly overpowered, and all the pirates were taken and brought to trial.

While they were in prison, Anne was allowed to visit Jack. She reputedly said, "I am sorry to see you there, but if you had fought like a man you need not be hang'd like a dog."

Rackham and the others were all hanged soon after. But Anne and Mary faced the judge and said, "My lord, we plead our bellies." That meant they were both pregnant and no judge would hang them, for that would have murdered the innocent child.

What happened after is purely the stuff of story. Some say that Mary was "seiz'd with a violent Fever . . . and died in Prison," and that Anne gave birth in the jail and was afterwards let go. Perhaps her father ransomed her. Or perhaps another man fell in love with her and paid her way out. No one will ever know for sure.

Rachel Wall

United States of America: late eighteenth century

Born in 1760 in Carlisle, Pennsylvania, Rachel Wall was raised on a prosperous farm. Her upbringing was rigid, with daily prayers and Bible readings on the Sabbath. This strict regimen griped Rachel, and when she was a teen she ran away from home. Though she returned, she soon ran away again, this time with a sailor, George Wall.

Sea Queens

For the first years of their marriage, Rachel worked as a housemaid on Boston's Beacon Hill, and George was a fisherman. But during the American Revolution, George served aboard a privateer. Suddenly the Walls saw piracy as a way of moving up in the world.

They stole a sloop in Essex and sailed toward Appledore Island, where they concocted a plan. Following each summer storm, they would tear down their sails and fly a distress signal. Rachel would stand at the rail, screaming until a passing boat stopped to help. Once the would-be rescuers came aboard, George and his crew of five murdered them.

From 1781 to 1782 the Walls collected six thousand dollars in cash—a huge sum then—and even more for the cargo, which they sold in

Rachel's Confession

The confession was published as a broadside entitled *Life, Last Words and Dying Confession of Rachel Wall Who, with William Smith and William Dunogan, was executed at Boston, on Thursday, October 8, 1789, for HIGH-WAY ROBBERY*. In the confession Rachel said, "I acknowledge myself to have been guilty of a great many crimes, such as Sabbath-breaking, stealing, lying, disobedience to parents, and almost every other sin a person could commit, except murder." And she ended, "And now, into the hands of Almighty God I commit my soul, relying on his mercy, through the merits and meditations of my Redeemer, and die an unworthy member of the Presbyterian Church, in the 29th year of my age."

Boston and Portsmouth. They killed twenty-four men along the way. The authorities thought that the pirated ships had all sunk in the storms that deviled the coast.

Ironically George drowned in a hurricane, and Rachel returned to work as a Beacon Hill maid. That proved too quiet—and underpaid—a life for Rachel. She went back to robbery, sneaking into ships docked in Boston Harbor and stealing from sailors as they slept. But she was caught and tried, not just for the robberies but also for an onboard murder. In prison she confessed all the facts about her life as a pirate. She was hanged on Boston Common on October 8, 1789, the last woman to be so punished.

Mary Anne Talbot

England: late eighteenth century

Mary Anne Talbot, born in 1778, went to sea disguised as a boy in 1792. She called herself John Taylor. Mary Anne worked as a servant to a British officer ordered to the West Indies. Neither the officer nor his superiors guessed that Mary Anne was a girl.

Later, when the regiment was ordered to Flanders, Mary Anne became a drummer under a different officer. But this officer guessed that she was a woman and kept her against her will. So one

From an Old Song

Put on a jolly sailor's dress
And daubed her hands with tar
To cross the raging sea
On board a man-of-war.

night Mary Anne deserted from the regiment and, disguised as a sailor, enlisted on a French ship.

That was a bad move. The ship turned out to be a privateer, quite often preying on British shipping. Because Mary Anne refused to fight against her own people, she was beaten severely.

Eventually the French privateer was attacked and overtaken by the English warship *Queen Charlotte*. When the British boarded the ship, Mary Anne begged to speak to the admiral. She told him that she was a poor British boy who was on the privateer innocently.

The admiral believed her and sent her to the *Brunswick,* where she was eventually promoted to principal cabin boy. But she was wounded in action, with grapeshot breaking the bone near her ankle and lodging in

Press Gangs

Only once did Mary Anne reveal that she was a woman. She'd been set upon by a press gang and she'd had enough of war by then.

Press is short for Impress Service. This was a British port organization dedicated to seizing men from eighteen to fifty-five to serve aboard the king's warships. Many a pirate had first been stolen by a press gang from his farm or workplace.

Grapeshot

Grapeshot was a type of ammunition that consisted of multiple round shot balls made of cast iron, lead, or other metals and was shot from a cannon.

her thigh just above her knee. She was treated both on the ship and later on shore. Either the doctors didn't discover that she was a girl, or more likely, in the heat of battle they didn't care.

Eventually she retired from the sea, collecting her naval pension. She didn't stop working altogether. Instead she joined a theater company and performed both male and female roles until her death at age thirty.

Who First Wrote About Mary Anne?

In 1804, just four years before she died, Mary Anne Talbot wrote her autobiography, as John Taylor. It was called *The Intrepid Female, or surprising life and adventures of Mary-Anne Talbot, otherwise John Taylor.* It appeared in Robert S. Kirby's book *Wonderful Museum* and said she was the illegitimate child of Lord Talbot.

Madame Ching

China: early nineteenth century

The most successful pirate in the world was a woman named Madame Ching, who sailed the South China Sea in the early 1800s.

Madame Ching married an old sailing captain, Ching I, in 1801. Because of a great famine in China, Ching I and his twelve sailors stole food. They were so successful that they began stealing silks, spices, and gold. Their one boat soon

Madame Ching's Names

Ching I Sao (meaning "wife of Ching")
Cheng I Sao (meaning "wife of Cheng")
Ching Yih Saou
Ching Shih
Shih Yang
His-Kai

became fifty boats. The mandarins—the government officials—sent a fleet of forty imperial ships after them. That was a mistake the mandarins would regret, for old Ching I and his men captured twenty-eight of the ships.

With his wife's help, Ching I managed to convince all the local pirates to band together and make him admiral of their fleet. They were now so numerous and pesky, they were called "wasps of the ocean." By 1804 Ching I ruled an association of four hundred junks with sixty thousand men under a constitution signed by seven pirate leaders.

They took to blockading rivers. Finally they captured some government warships that had ten to fifteen cannons each. They were so successful that shipping came to a standstill, and the pirates began ransacking inland. Their fleet had grown to eight hundred large ships, one thousand smaller ones, and over sixty-five thousand men.

But on November 16, 1807, old Ching I died—some

Life on Chinese Ships

Chinese ships called junks were often home to an entire community, a kind of floating village. The women of the junk community were as capable sailors as their husbands, working by their men's sides in both fishing and trading, and, it turns out, pirating. As Lieutenant Glasspoole observed, the junks were "filled with their families, men, women, and children."

say he drowned in a gale, others that he was captured and tortured to death. His wife took over his command. This was not as uncommon as it sounds. In the Chinese pirate communities, women often fought side by side with their husbands and even commanded ships.

Madame Ching married her dead husband's second-in-command, a man named Ch'ang P'aou. She made him head of her red squadron and so he became her spokesman in all things. By now Madame Ching commanded a total of two thousand boats and seventy thousand men, the most any pirate in the world ever led.

We know much about her because in 1809 she captured a young officer in the East India Company—Richard Glasspoole—and his men. He wrote about his adventures in the book *Mr. Glasspoole and the Chinese Pirates,* though the book was not published for years.

Glasspoole mistook Madame Ching for a man, writ-

> **Dividing the Fleet**
>
> Ching I's fleet was divided into six squadrons. Each squadron had its own special cruising area and its own colored banner. A lieutenant commander was in charge of each squadron. The yellow squadron was ruled by Scourge of the Eastern Sea; the white by Jewel of the Whole Crew; black by O-po-tae; green by Frog's Meal; and blue by Bird and Stone. The sixth was Ching I's personal squadron, sailing under the red banner.

ing, "I was then taken to the chief. He was seated on the deck of a large chair, dressed in purple silk with a black turban on; He appeared to be about thirty years of age, a stout, commanding-looking gentleman." It is not clear if Glasspoole ever understood his mistake, though from a Western perspective it was not surprising. In Glasspoole's native England, having a woman commanding such a fleet would have been unthinkable. Later he would say that she was "daring and enterprising."

The emperor of China was extremely angry with the pirates, so he sent his best admirals to try to defeat them. The first of these battles, with the venerable mandarin Kwo Lang Lin, was a success for the pirates. Madame Ching was ready for him, sending the red squadron under P'aou's command into a sheltered bay to wait as bait. Then she led the rest of her fleet in behind the mandarin, boxing him in. He committed suicide in shame.

The second battle, in 1808, was a disaster at first.

Ching I's Death

"On the seventeenth day of the tenth moon in the twentieth year of Kea-King," the chroniclers reported, a great hurricane—called a typhoon—drowned Ching I and hundreds of his men, who were on a raid.

Madame Ching

Admiral Tsuen Mow Sun came upon one of the pirate squadrons alone and, with his one hundred warships, destroyed them. Then the admiral's men celebrated—a grave mistake on their part. Gathering the rest of her fleet, Madame Ching advanced on the celebrating imperial force. One by one she captured the boats and set them afire. As a survivor wrote: "Our fleet was scattered, thrown into disorder, and consequently cut to pieces."

Upon the advice of his ministers, the emperor decided

Typical Pirate Ship

Glasspoole wrote that "the afterpart [stern] is appropriated to the captain and his wives; he generally has five or six. Every man is allowed a small berth about four feet square, where he stows his wife and family."

As for the chief's junk, it had thirty-eight guns, according to Glasspoole. The guns were mounted on carriages and secured by a rope around the muzzle, which was then threaded through a hole in the ship's side. This made the guns very moveable, and during any fight the deck was stripped and kept wet so the guns could swivel easily.

Sea Queens

to starve Madame Ching out. He ordered his ships kept in port with the hope that, having no ships to prey on, the pirates would have no other option but to surrender. But Madam Ching sent her band far up the Canton River tributaries to conquer the cities and towns.

Being desperate, the emperor offered a pardon to any pirate who would surrender. He offered money, safety, and a retirement home besides. Madame Ching laughed at the offer, as did her husband, P'aou. But O-po-tae, the commander of the black squadron, accepted the offer, taking with him 160 ships.

The emperor then used O-po-tae as a spokesman, and slowly many other pirates left. Even P'aou finally took the emperor's pardon, saying, "We pirates are like broken bamboo canes on the sea, floating and sinking alternately without thought of rest."

Protection Racket

Most of Madame Ching's money came from "contributions" that towns and villages along the Pearl River paid to be "protected" from pirates. After each payday a great feast with opium smoking and gambling was held.

Ransom

Another way the pirates found to make money was to hold people for ransom. Glasspoole and his men were ransomed by the East India Company for 1,915 pounds sterling, two chests of gunpowder, two chests of opium, and a telescope. That was an enormous sum for that time.

Madame Ching

P'aou was allowed to keep a private squadron of twenty junks.

O-po-tae and his men were each given farmland on which to settle.

As for Madame Ching, she left pirating when it was clear she had no other choice. By the end of 1810, the great body of pirates had been disbanded. The chroniclers wrote: "All is quiet on the rivers and the four seas are tranquil and people live in peace and plenty."

And Madame Ching? Some say she turned to smuggling, others that she ran a gambling house in Canton and died in 1844 at the age of sixty. Still other reports have it that she married the governor and became a lady.

Madame Ching's Rules

A man who goes alone on shore will have his ears slit in the presence of the entire fleet. A repeat of this action—and he will be executed.

No pirate may take a woman without her consent, nor wed her without permission of his chief officer. To do so means instant death.

In a march through the countryside, any man advancing or retreating without orders will be beheaded.

Not even the smallest object may be privately removed from the common loot. Every piece must be accurately registered. From every ten pieces, the individual receives two. The remaining eight parts goes to the warehouse for common stock. Any stealing from the captured booty will be punishable by death.

Captured women and children will no longer be hanged by their hair from the ships.

Roundup

Here are some other women pirates—though not an exhaustive list—about whom little is known. Most pirates—men or women—have remained unknown to history unless captured and hanged or pardoned. Also the earlier accounts have been so compromised by folklore and legend, there are often few facts to back up the stories we do have. This list is just to remind the reader that women pirates may have been few in number, but they have appeared in just about every country and time when pirating was a scourge on the seas.

I have only listed women pirates about whom we know more than just a name.

Sea Queens

PRINCESS SELA—About 420, Norwegian Viking, sister to Norwegian king Kolles, also a pirate, who was her greatest enemy as well.

RUSLA—Possibly ninth century, Norwegian princess who, furious with her brother, King Tesdondus, for losing his crown to the Danes, plundered up and down the Danish coast till her brother sank her ship. When she swam away from the wreckage, he had his sailors beat her to death with their oars.

RUSSILA AND HER SISTER STIKLA—Possibly ninth century, Norwegian Vikings who led an organization of pirates that plagued the Dutch baron Hirwitto.

SIDA AL HURRA—sixteenth century Muslim Barbary pirate and for thirty years the regent of the western coast of Morocco. Known as the Steerswoman of Tetuan.

JACQUOTTE DELAHAYE—1656–1660s, Caribbean buccaneer who commanded one hundred men.

MADAME DE FRESNE—late 1600s, French marquess kidnapped by a corsair, later married him.

Roundup

MARY HARVEY OR HARLEY—1726, Virginia, pirated along with three men. They got the death sentence but she was released.

SARAH BISHOP—1778–1780, a New Yorker who was forced to join the crew of a British privateer during the American Revolution.

CATHERINE HAGERTY AND CHARLOTTE BADGER—1806, Australia, part of a group of convicts who seized a colonial brig, *Venus*, docked at Port Dalrymple. The pirates then sailed for New Zealand, where Hagerty died in April 1807. Charlotte and her child remained on shore, living with local Maori people a while before boarding a ship and escaping to Tonga.

GERTRUDE IMOGENE STUBBS, Canada—1898–1903, also known as "Gunpowder Gertie, the Pirate Queen of the Kootenays," sailed on the British Columbian lake, Kootenay, and its river system.

Sea Queens

The Sweet Trade

Pirates called pirating "the sweet trade," and it is not surprising that girls and women throughout the centuries took part in it. After all, they already went disguised as boys into the navies and armies around the world, so why not into pirating as well?

Of course, there is so much storytelling, exaggeration, and just plain lying about the pirating trade that it's hard to say with absolute certainty that all the women pirates on these pages are real. I have tried to stick with those that most scholars agree actually lived. Except . . . except even the real ones have hugely exaggerated exploits attached to their names. It seems that old tars—old sailors—do tend to tell big yarns.

Bibliography

When I wrote an earlier book on women pirates, there was little easily obtained information about them. I didn't know then about Grania O'Malley, or Artemisia, or Teuta. In the over forty years since publication of that book, *Pirates in Petticoats*, scholars have done much work on the subject of women pirates. This book uses a lot of that new material.

Bibliography

Books

American Heritage. *Pirates of the Spanish Main.* New York: American Heritage Publishing Co., Inc., 1961.

Besson, Maurice. *The Scourge of the Indies.* New York: Random House, 1929.

Brooke, Henry K. *Book of Pirates.* Philadelphia: J. B. Perry, 1841.

Cabal, Joan. *Piracy and Pirates: A History. Translated from the Spanish by James Cleugh.* London: Jarrolds Publishers, 1957.

Carse, Robert. *The Age of Piracy.* New York: Rinehart & Winston, 1957.

Chambers, Ann. Granuaile: *The Life and Times of Grace O'Malley c. 1530–1603.* Dublin, Ireland: Wolfhound Press, 1988.

Cordingly, David. *Under the Black Flag: The Romance and the Reality of Life Among the Pirates.* New York: Random House, 1995.

Driscoll, Charles B. *Pirates, Ahoy!* Syndicated column, June 15, 1928; July 22, 1928; September 25, 1932; November 20, 1932; November 26, 1933.

Druett, Joan. *She Captains: Heroines and Hellions of the Sea.* New York: Simon & Schuster, 2000.

Sea Queens

Fuller, Basil, and Ronald Leslie-Melville. *Pirate Harbours and Their Secrets*. London: Stanley Paul & Company Ltd., 1935.

Glasspoole, Richard. *Mr. Glasspoole and the Chinese Pirates*. London: Golden Cockerel Press, 1935.

Gollomb, Joseph. *Pirates Old and New*. London: Selwyn & Blount, Ltd., 1931.

Gosse, Philip. *The History of Piracy*. London: Longmans, Green & Company, 1932.

Johnson, Captain Charles. *A General History of the Robberies and Murders of the Most Notorious Pirates*. London: Routledge & Kegan Paul, Ltd., 1926, 1955.

Johnson, Cathy. *Pyrates in Petticoats: A fanciful & factual history of the legends, tales, and exploits of the most notorious female pirates*. Excelsior Springs, MO: Graphics/Fine Arts Press, 2000.

Kemp, P. K., and Christopher Lloyd. *Brethren of the Coast: Buccaneers of the South Seas*. New York: St. Martin's Press, 1961.

Klausmann, Ulrike, Marion Meinzerin, and Gabriel Kuhn. *Women Pirates and the Politics of the Jolly Roger*. Montreal: Black Rose Books, 1997.

Lilius, Aleko. *I Sailed with Chinese Pirates*. London: Arrowsmith, 1930.

MacLeish, Fleming, and Martin Krieger. *The Privateers*. New York: Random House, 1962.

Bibliography

Mathew, David. *"Cornish and Welsh Pirates in the Reign of Elizabeth."* English Historical Revue, July 1924.

Pringle, Patrick. *Jolly Roger.* New York: W. W. Norton, 1953.

Rediker, Marcus. *Between the Devil and the Deep Blue Sea: Merchant Seamen, Pirates, and the Anglo-American Maritime World 1700–1750.* Cambridge: Cambridge University Press, 1987.

Sherry, Frank. *Raiders & Rebels: The Golden Age of Piracy.* New York: Quill/William Morrow, 1986.

Snow, Edward Rowe. *Piracy, Mutiny and Murder.* New York: Dodd, Mead & Co., 1959.

Snow, Edward Rowe. *Women of the Sea.* New York: Dodd, Mead & Co., 1962.

Whitley, H. M. *"Dame Killigrew and the Spanish Ship."* Journal of the Royal Institution of Cornwall, July 1883.

Wilkes, John. *The Illyrians.* Oxford, UK, and Cambridge, MA: Blackwell Press, 1995.

Worth, R. N. *"The Family of Killigrew."* Journal of the Royal Institution of Cornwall, April 1871.

Yolen, Jane. *Pirates in Petticoats.* New York: David McKay Company, Inc., 1963.

Sea Queens

Helpful websites

http://www.tallgirlshorts.net/marymary/caroline.html

This site is an interview with a student in a women's studies
master's program who shares her research on Grace O'Malley.

http://www.rootsweb.com/~nwa/grace.html

This is a biography of Grace O'Malley and is a good starting
place for information.

http://www.bonaventure.org.uk/ed/deberry.htm

This has information on Charlotte de Berry's life and career as
a pirate. There are links to other sites dealing with pirates
and strong women.

Index

Index

Sea Queens

Index

Some of the greatest pirates ever known were women.

Jane Yolen is the award-winning author of nearly three hundred children's books, including picture books, fiction, nonfiction, fantasy, science fiction, and poetry. She has been called the Hans Christian Andersen of America. She lives in western Massachusetts and in Scotland, and travels widely speaking at conferences and children's literature events.

Christine Joy Pratt majored in fine art at the University of Vermont. After taking up illustration, she bought a one-way ticket to Hawai'i and has never looked back. Her work has appeared in *Cricket* and *Spider* magazines. She is the illustrator of *This Is America: The American Spirit in Places and People*.